DISCONSOLATE DREAMERS: ON PESSIMISM AND UTOPIA

Rachid M'Rabty

T0015160

Winchester, UK
Washington, USA

JOHN HUNT PUBLISHING

First published by Zero Books, 2024
Zero Books is an imprint of John Hunt Publishing Ltd., No. 3 East St.,
Alresford,
Hampshire SO24 9EE, UK
office@jhpbooks.com
www.johnhuntpublishing.com
www.zero-books.net

For distributor details and how to order please visit the 'Ordering' section
on our website.

Text copyright: Rachid M'Rabty 2023

Paperback ISBN: 978 1 80341 326 6
eBook ISBN: 978 1 80341 494 2
PCN: 2023930467

A CIP catalogue record for this book is available from the British Library.

Design credit(s): Lapiz Digital

UK: Printed and bound by CPI Group (UK) Ltd, Croydon, CR0 4YY
Printed in North America by CPI GPS partners

We operate a distinctive and ethical publishing philosophy in
all areas of our business, from our global network of authors to
production and worldwide distribution.

TABLE OF CONTENTS

INTRODUCTION

It is 2023, and we have lived through a recent history rife with disillusionment and horror. We are aware of the pernicious nature of optimism, more increasingly attuned to the paradoxes and the contradictions of the positivist outlook within the cultural arrangement of postmodern capitalism, and we are increasingly sceptical of happy endings. Hopelessness, the shrug of disaffection and frustration are now evermore present on our collective horizon. This shared, disappointing experience confirms that, now more than ever, the strategies of resistance and the optimism that so often characterises radical discourse seem increasingly doomed to failure, as we are resigned to a slow and painful descent into the meat-grinder that is capitalism. This short book, however, is not a lament on hopelessness — despite what presumptions may be drawn from its title. This book presents, instead, a speculative rumination on how the Left might re-enthuse its own critical toolkit, how it might provoke — revive even — a sense of urgency, via a more welcoming engagement with pessimism, as new utopian alternatives and paradigms are sought.

By wielding pessimism as a critical device, this book implores a rethinking of the experiential narrative (of how we experience the world around us, the stories we tell ourselves about how life is or can be, and the meaning that we give our actions and thoughts within this paradigm) by offering a critical mirror against life lived under the hegemony, power and machinations of modern-day capitalism. As the pages that follow suggest, to think speculatively and critically against modern-day capitalism is also to individually and collectively disavow the perverse optimism which sustains it. Through the pessimistic position (one that does not shy away from the full scale of the predicament facing us), we can begin to think about different alternatives. Whether found in quiet acts of naysaying to the world, in nihilistic, self-destructive or self-effacing radicalism, or in wider-ranging renegotiations of the acceptable and the possible at the limit of reason, pessimism beckons forth the possibility for alternatives or destinations that — though perhaps disconcerting or antithetical — reveal, to some degree, the utopian dream of the *impossible place*.

By questioning the extent to which optimism should be dispensed of in favour of a pragmatic and critical pessimism, eschatological fantasies of escape and alterity can be explored, and their possibilities adopted in our collective lament and response to the present. In this vein, the ideas which follow stem from a particular question (or more accurately, a fragmented series of questions): How can we fake optimism any longer? To what extent can pessimism be recuperated in purposeful gesture or praxis? Then, finally, in a world devoid of 'rational' or 'viable' alternatives, to what extent does the pessimist reveal a radical or speculative version of 'utopian' alterity in the twenty-first century?

In anticipation of and in response to some of these questions, I explore the extent to which pessimism is compatible with a radical utopian goal — namely, the desire for an escape or an inoculation from the horror of modern existence — and highlight how pessimism inspires critical interventions against the system in the form of utopian ideas and radical projections. As this book speculates, in a thoroughly hopeless world devoid of rational or viable alternatives, it is time now to turn to the disconsolate, to the pessimist, for a glimpse of utopian alterity, or as Slavoj Žižek states: 'It is only when we despair and don't know any more what to do that change can be enacted — we have to go through this zero point of hopelessness'.[1]

Debunking the synonymous correlation that presently exists between neoliberal capitalism and cultural/societal progressivism, I critique the intolerable, optimistic delusion that the steer and drive of capitalism (and its political apparatus) leads to a utopian better future. In so doing, I consider pessimism as a pragmatic, galvanising starting point for the reconsideration of utopia as an engendered negation and utopianism as a call for disentanglement, escape or change, rather than the extension or completion of existing neoliberal capitalist hegemony. In so doing, I show that pessimism does not void utopianism — on the contrary — it clears the way for its conception and emergence; it necessitates it.

1. A NOTE AGAINST OPTIMISM

To be clear from the outset, the arguments contained in the following pages follow a central conceit: that optimism is a charade, its true beneficiaries being those in power, such as the political, economic and spiritual demagogues of the twenty-first century, in whose sole interest it remains to uphold the façade of a world being capably steered toward a brighter tomorrow. Optimism is void as a means of coping with the tangible, experiential nightmare of the lived experience for the majority of those not in power. The notion that positivity equates to an enlightened rationality is exposed on a scale ranging from perverse naivety to downright sadistic and callous disregard. The optimist takes no responsibility for the present and future. Indeed, optimism is a sedative, nulling the pain and horror of existence with an illogical deferral to an unsubstantiated, brighter future. By contrast, the pessimist is inherently engaged in the business of exposure and critique. As such, if we at all claim to be interested in utopian visions of alterity or anti-capitalist action (which should go hand in hand), then we must disentangle the inaccurate and synonymous links between optimism and utopia, redeem pessimism as more than a shallow, callow and miserabilist temperament, and ultimately dispense of the optimistic outlook for a pragmatic and radical pessimism.

Eugene Thacker calls pessimism 'the philosophical form of disenchantment', and as a philosophical frame through which to view and participate in the world, admittedly, pessimism is not always ideal.[2] As the critics Stoneman and Packer argue:

> Even if pessimists found an audience willing to entertain
> their ideas, they would still face another significant hurdle,
> namely, that the denial of existential significance is at some
> odds with the affirmative function of rhetoric to preserve
> a world of meaning, one in which material reality is not
> blindly cruel and indifferent but welcoming, reassuring and
> kind.[3]

However, it is conspicuous that today some of the most apocalyptic and reprehensible aspects of social and political coercion come wrapped in or justified by a rhetoric of optimism and progress — all of which neglects to address or knowingly obfuscates an underlying malicious intent. Lauren Berlant, Slavoj Žižek and Terry Eagleton have each, over the past decade, presented differing but provocative and noteworthy additions to the ever-expanding library of anti-optimistic discourse. For each of these critics, optimism is lambasted as a cruel staple of social and political experience that is an obstacle to your flourishing, as the ideological scaffold of an enforced neoliberal capitalist hegemony and, perhaps most damningly, as a barrier to radical action.[4] In recent years, each has launched an attack on the core principles of optimism that errs towards the side of a recuperation of pessimism as the logical and pragmatic, radical or inevitable ethical direction.

Slavoj Žižek, in *The Courage of Hopelessness* (2017) articulates his own preference to be a pessimist: 'not expecting anything' mean that 'here and there [one is] nicely surprised', rather than the perpetual witness to one's hopes and dreams being dashed all of the time.[5] Žižek proceeds to describe a world in which catastrophe and terror are renormalised so that the possibility they can stimulate and motivate any cathartic, radical response is negated. The result is, then, tragically, the cultivation and forceful application of the neoliberal capitalist consensus and the further attrition and denigration of the Left. 'The power edifice', he argues, has 'demonstrated an extra-ordinary ability to use movements of contestation as a source of its own renovation', resulting in a hopeless situation when the optimist's so-called better future masks the descent towards catastrophe with small acts of 'modest reformism'.[6] Modest reformism might be better for PR than impending annihilation, but it certainly does stifle any rational, pragmatic and serious debate or the implementation of threatening and rigorous structural improvement. By this narrative, optimism accepts those small, marginal, token gains as proof that a better future is on its way. But, in doing so, it defers the necessity of real, tangible action that threatens this. Reform, or working within a system to better or improve it, is for Žižek the truest sign of the Left's failure and, he argues, is even more perilous because it detracts from the pursuit of a full-blown revolutionary break. For Žižek, neoliberal capitalism utilises a perverse mechanisation and application of utopian ideology to project itself as the pinnacle of human socio-political organisation. For those interested in maintaining this pretence, it is only the lack of total commitment to this ideal that is the cause of imperfection, and final-form utopian capitalism is the remedy to human social and cultural imperfection. What Žižek alludes to, however, is that this is not utopian thought at all, but a violent perversion, as (a particular projection of) utopia becomes the ideological scaffold legitimising and holding up neoliberal hegemony, and that this can only be overcome through a turn to 'communism', which in Žižek's work resembles a speculative exercise in utopian negativism precisely because it is not the design of a tangible structure that holds, but an abstract disruption that collapses the perverse pretence into nothingness.

As Žižek argues, we must accept (and encourage) the challenging of optimistic idealism as a necessity. Threat, he offers, is our unavoidable fate within our current inescapable hegemon. Though we can attempt to mitigate risk, choose to be careful and strive to make little steps toward marginal improvements, we are ultimately doomed: fated to destruction within the capitalist system. His solution, then, in typically bombastic style, is 'not to be very careful', (as such care supplants us as unwitting participants on the road leading to disaster) but to abandon any predilections or presumptions of a better tomorrow, and 'become fully aware of the explosive set of interconnections that makes the entire situation dangerous'.[7] Only in doing so, in opening our eyes critically to the damaging and catastrophic nature of idealism and faith in the social, economic, political and even moral codes and structures under which we live our lives, can we begin to embark on the really difficult work of undermining, changing or escaping the coordinates of this world.

Such damaging idealism, likewise, for Lauren Berlant, in her influential and provocative study *Cruel Optimism* (2011), is a position (or thought trap) that needs to be overcome or recast in order for the human to thrive going forward. Ultimately, for Berlant, optimism is a cruel fantasy and an 'obstacle to your flourishing'.[8] Optimism is undesirable as it serves to maintain an impossible relation — that of the subject to a fantasy or idealism, which is itself inherently tied to cultural and political ideals of capitalism in Western European and North American culture and society — that ultimately frays into, amongst other things, depression, dissociation and cynicism as ordinary life and the 'good life' fantasy becomes overwhelmed and denigrated from each crisis to the next.[9] Whether it be the belief in a utopian political project or the harbouring of idyllic values pertaining to the promise of upward mobility, equality, security and intimacy or real human connection, the mechanics and manifestation of the positivist attachment we hold to and invest in these kinds of fantasies becomes attritional; it impedes us, grinds us down. Cruel optimism reflects the relation between fantasy (the life we aim for and project towards) and futility (the life/lives we live) in which our experience

4

(specifically, for Berlant, within American and Western European societies) is one of a dependency, necessitating the drive towards the nebulous fulfilment of the abstract fantasy — or, to speak its name, the continuity of neoliberal capitalism. It is a fantasy which is irrational, affective (plays on feeling rather than meaning and judgement), and its cruelty stems from the fact that it inhibits and prevents any rational, critical dialogue with self and society that may be more beneficial to your own and a wider societal sense of compassion, fulfilment or betterment.

Optimism, for Berlant, binds subjects to ideas with deleterious consequences. While optimism suggests the ultimate realisation of the 'satisfying thing' is possible, the cruelty of this suggestion becomes apparent when we realise the fallacy of realising this in actuality or come to recognise the full extent or cost of this attachment within a specific ideological, cultural or relational context. Cruel optimism, then, is the name given to represent the intricate synthesis of desiring attachment and existential insecurity weaponised and deployed to further tie us up within, in a masochistic, unending, relational bind within the parameters of social convention or a power-structure, wherein humans are condemned to live out their lives in a perpetual cycle of striving and frustration. And with each failure or disappointment comes not a questioning, refusal or detachment, but a more determined investment in the fantasy (and system) itself: 'I lost my house because I did not work hard enough...', 'I am not happy because I do not have all the expensive nice things...', and so forth.

Cruel optimism, in this sense, recalls the Marxist notion of false consciousness, whereby exploitative capitalist ideology creates self-sustaining myths and fantasies that demarcate the parameters of what is possible within its illusory reality, whilst masking the privitisation of power and rampant abuses that sustain this. Optimism, similarly, manipulates sensation and emotion to provoke movement or continuity within a system or culture, whilst simultaneously obfuscating the fact of our real impasse within the inescapable parameters of the cultural-economic capitalist hegemon. Berlant's charting of cruel optimism as an affective, relational force in how the subject interacts with and participates in the world demonstrates how utopian notions of 'the good-life fantasy' are underpinned by a cycle of attachment, disappointment and subsequent recalibration of our commitment to the fantasy-idea or object that is cruel: first, in cultivating the conditions of our own disappointment as we inevitably fail to meet utopian ideals within the neoliberal context; and secondly, in further binding us to this nefarious relationship, wherein our satisfactions, accomplishments, value and worth are valid only within the context of the fantasy-system that provides their meaning.

As *Cruel Optimism* demonstrates, ours is a situation which is sustained by an optimistic assumption/belief that the prevailing 'liberal democratic' capitalist system will lead to progress, security, upward mobility, equality and so on as a consequence of the almost-divine providence of economic forces to stimulate growth, prosperity and betterment for all. These assumptions, however, are fraying, as is our trust and belief in capitalist society to 'reliably provide opportunities for individuals to carve out relations of reciprocity that seem fair and that foster life as a project of adding up to something'.[10] Whilst optimism sustains these utopian ideals and the social/behavioural contract between subject and society, a growing pessimism takes hold as we become sceptical towards this and recognise the pernicious cruelty of this particularly one-sided relationship. This is something which Terry Eagleton's persuasive and eminently readable *Hope without Optimism* (2015) further examines.

If life exists as trauma, and progress, betterment or fulfilment is grounded in catastrophe, as Eagleton recalls from Walter Benjamin, then the optimist is incapable of facilitating progress, nor are they capable of genuine hope or compassion, since they deny the very conditions that necessitate its being. In this way, optimism is fatalistic: a terminal fallacy to be discarded at the earliest opportunity. Walter Benjamin, to whom Eagleton turns toward on this point, is likewise not a big believer in optimistic notions of 'progress', as he recalls that the continuity of history is inherently not a good thing and to expect 'better' is to trust too much in a system or cultural logic that has thus far not proven itself worthy of our confidence. Against optimism, Benjamin instead reserves hope for a somewhat messianic eruption that will entirely break and release us from the trap of historical continuity — hope for a complete negation from the paradigms of the world as we know it.

If Benjamin is the hopeful pessimist, Ernst Bloch, author of the encyclopaedic *The Principle of Hope* (1954), is the preeminent hopeful optimist of Marxism. Bloch is a figure somewhat overlooked by contemporary Marxist criticism, who argued that hope is built into the universe and is the basis of all that is positive within the human spirit. For Karl Marx, progress and suffering are inherently linked, though for Ernst Bloch, this suffering is redeemed by an optimistic belief that the trials and tribulations of history pave the way toward something better. In this sense, for Bloch at least, hope is ingrained in the procession and movement of time and history, and this perpetual movement beyond the instances and events of suffering is cause to celebrate. In doing so, however, Bloch invites us to believe in a more positive future to an unreasonable and impractical degree. For Eagleton, such hopeful optimism is unpalatable. It risks too much in its passing over and failure to sufficiently consider the bad to its full extent, and more still, that this unreasonable optimism can only lead to further disappointment and disaffection down the line as optimistic expectancy fails to materialise.[11]

Often considered the most utopian of Marxists, Bloch's writing called for a concrete and tangible utopia, a utopia that is both realistic and grounded in doable social improvement. However, such calls for a concrete utopia do beg the question as to whether it is really utopian thinking or just action doomed to ideological compromise within the parameters of the current world? Eagleton, here, questions Bloch's fundamental optimism by quite rightly pointing out that hope in and of itself is absolutely no guarantee of betterment or alternative coming into fulfilment, and so, while we may remain or strive to be hopeful, hope must not fall the way of optimistic complacency — expectation. There is, then, a realisation that the utopian 'better' requires some radical dissonance beginning with a rethinking of what is deemed a success or failure, and an acceptance that whilst accomplishments may not be seen in one's lifetime or in concrete terms, this does not negate the poignancy or necessity of the action for all. As Eagleton recalls, 'not to succeed in the end is not necessarily to have failed', for 'unless one combats the inevitable, one will never know how inevitable it was in the first place'.[12]

Raymond Williams, the esteemed British Marxist literary and cultural critic, argued in *The Politics of Modernism* (1989), that

> [t]he fact is that neither the frankly utopian form, nor the even more qualified outlines of practicable futures can begin to flow until we have faced, at this necessary depth, the divisions and contradictions which now inhibit them.[13]

In this sentiment, Eagleton agrees, as *Hope Without Optimism* ultimately posits that any radical break or challenge to the contemporary paradigm values must begin with a critical dissensus and acknowledgement that the worst is an opponent we cannot overlook. As he concludes, 'the worst is in some perverse sense a source of hope, bringing as it does the assurance that one can sink no further'.[14] Whereas optimism achieves nothing, hope offers a reckoning of what the future could be. Amidst the tragedy of our situation, hope is what survives the general ruin and catastrophe. It is not a fanatical optimistic belief that change or affirmation will come, but an enduring radical belief (bordering desire) that a path out of our tragic state may yet be attainable — even if this presents itself as a visceral and profound nothingness. But nonetheless, as Eagleton alludes, even a ghostly silence is poignantly transformative of the chaos and noise that precedes it.

The difficulties faced by those on the Left in their attempts to transition hope into concrete practical action and the development of something new should not be seen as a failure but as the tragic consequence of a widespread cultural inability to see a viable pathway beyond the structural foundations of the present hegemon. Underpinning Eagleton's intervention is the recognition of the necessity of tragedy, that is — the necessity in recognising that something has gone drastically wrong irrespective of the intention, which we must haul ourselves through 'to achieve a modicum of well-being'.[15]

Eagleton's reading against optimism centres on the distinction between (and synonymous decoupling of) optimism and hope, as being eminently necessary. Hope is the drive or call to action through our catastrophic wastelands, towards what *could* be, without the sense of knowing what is to come. By contrast, optimism is to hold that what *could* be *will* be, which has no tangible basis. As Eagleton concludes, we are, in our present situation, befallen by a certain tragedy, but our disconsolation in this realisation presents a necessary starting point on our quest to understand and respond to the cruel optimism of the contemporary and reclaim a discourse of utopian alterity.

2. A NOTE ON PESSIMISM

In the common imagination, to be pessimistic (in the most extreme sense) is to refuse the supposedly rational discourses that underpin our culture and regulate our behaviour as 'good' citizens and human beings. It is to cast off the shackles of our unsavoury intellect and, ultimately, to allow oneself to confront and take control of the one and only meaningful choice that life presents: whether to go on living, or not. In this sense, the pessimist refuses the comfort and privilege of a world-for-us that 'morality' and human egocentrism have afforded us. Pessimism, in this most fatalistic reading, incites a horrific contention, one that questions the fundamental failure of rational thinking, logic and structure/order to achieve the desired measure of contrition or relief from the horror of existence. This view is argued throughout esteemed horror and weird fiction author Thomas Ligotti's impassioned defence of pessimism *The Conspiracy against the Human Race* (2010).[16] For Ligotti, things went downhill for us all as a species as soon as we human beings became self-aware; or to paraphrase a particularly pessimistic retort, our consciousness is the parent of all horrors. In response to this, at the nascency of human awareness, human beings have clung to their optimism as they have endeavoured to create some grand narrative, meaning or means of understanding a world in which they have purpose. Thus, a persistent critique that counters the generally held pessimistic viewpoint is that the underlying denial or refutation of existential significance is in direct contrivance of how the majority of people (and the structural forces that govern and shape societies) choose to affirm life as wholly worthwhile and committed to processes of betterment that elevate society through reason and meaning.

Of all philosophical figures, none have cast as large a shadow over the critical understanding of pessimism than the curmudgeonly nineteenth-century German philosopher Arthur Schopenhauer. A curious and not particularly likeable man, his essay 'On Women' reveals him as a raging misogynist with some unresolved maternal issues, though he was also a prodigious and ambitious thinker who provocatively railed against Western intellectualism's succumbing to the tenants of a thriving German idealism. The poster boy of nineteenth-century philosophical and metaphysical pessimism, for Schopenhauer, the world exists and is experienced as two interlinked but very distinct phases: first, as 'Representation'; and second, as 'Will'.[17] The former refers to life as a specifically phenomenological experience (more generally understood as how the world appears and is experienced by us, the living human subject), whilst the latter refers to the proto-unconscious, instinctive and unrepresentable driving force which, though 'felt' and impactful, cannot be grasped at. It is the experience of the world beyond our comprehension: the world as it truly is beyond the unnatural frame and limitations of human perceptibility and understanding. 'Will', to some extent, resembles the impossible world — impossible in that, by strictly experiential human standards, it will forever be beyond us. What is not beyond us, however, for Schopenhauer at least, is the ability to recognise this traumatic disjuncture and our ability to comprehend of life and existence as pain and suffering, boredom, indifference and meaninglessness.

In 'On the Suffering of the World', taken from *Parerga and Paralipomena* (1851), Arthur Schopenhauer writes:

If suffering is not the first immediate object of our life, then our existence is the most inexpedient and inappropriate thing in the world. For it is absurd to assume that the infinite pain, which everywhere abounds in the world and springs from the want and misery essential to life, could be purposeless and purely accidental. Our susceptibility to pain is well-nigh infinite; but that to pleasure has narrow limits. It is true that each separate piece of misfortune seems to be an exception, but misfortune in general is the rule.[18]

Pessimism, for Schopenhauer, is a natural, pragmatic response to a world marked by suffering. Furthermore, as he describes in *The World as Will and Representation* (1819, 1844), his abject cynicism and fundamental negativism stems from an understanding of our torturous existential predicament, and that (our) life and the decisions we make only further accentuate this as we unintentionally or inadvertently exercise the fulfilment of 'Will'. Every decision made serves the Will's agenda — or the 'Will to life' — be it survival, nourishment, reproduction, or capacity for knowledge. It is an agenda that serves only the continuation of life and thus of the continuation of our ever-suffering existential condition. It is little surprise that Schopenhauer's pessimistic determinism has been tremendously off-putting to many readers, both in his own era and our own (though, curiously, he has found a committed audience for his imaginative and speculative philosophical provocations within weird fiction, horror and speculative literary and philosophical circles). His poster-boy status amongst some philosophical and literary circles, however, has done little to temper (and indeed may have only further accentuated) his caricature as a misanthropic doom-monger, peddling metaphysical inconsistencies whilst throwing insults at Hegel. To a degree, this description rings true; there is, however, an often overlooked or dismissed value in reading Schopenhauer as — brace yourself — a fundamental moralist, concerned not in wallowing in his bleak lot (and, of course, philosophers do not wallow in any case; they brood, melancholically), but in articulating a more critical understanding of the ever-suffering human condition, a certain (I hesitate...) compassion even.

To the scorn of the more optimistically attuned reader, Schopenhauer posits that all earthly pleasures, satisfactions, respite and relief are only possible, retaining any value whatsoever, in relation to some negative that precedes it, and to which it exists to placate. To borrow a much-hackneyed Schopenhauerism, everything is borne of suffering. In this, nothing positive can exist in isolation as it is always a response to the negative — specifically, of an existential and experiential pain of anguish. In dialectical terms, pain is the tangible, felt presence or existent, whereas satisfaction (and all associated feelings or notions) is the absence — the non-existence — of said *a priori* existent: an intangible ideal, in a similar relation to how utopia emerges as the 'curative'; 'satisfaction', but also as the incorporeal, non-existent negation. Though despite all the associated naysaying and propagation of life's fundamental and unrelenting meaninglessness, Schopenhauer isn't advocating his readership march themselves en masse off Alte Brücke and into the river Main in despair (though admittedly, due to Schopenhauer's immense unpopularity in his own day, there probably would not have been much of a mass following, so to speak, anyway). Furthermore, pessimism more roundly, and contrary to popular belief, does not inevitably tread the path to self-destructive or suicidal ideations. Granted, for many pessimists it is true that no other alternative or respite seems enough; in the grand scheme of things, the endgame need not be an end to life. E.M. Cioran, along with Nietzsche, Schopenhauer and, more recently, David Benatar, Eugene Thacker and Simon Critchley have all posited a rendition on the belief that, ultimately, suicide is too optimistic — 'too positive and assertive, too caught up in the fantasy of salvation through death'.[19] Likewise, Thomas Ligotti, in *The Conspiracy Against the Human Race,* posits that suicide is not the answer to the disconsolation of the existing subject, nor their suffering as (ab) used subject of capitalist/corporate societies. What Schopenhauer, in his own charmingly bleak way, is calling for is a pragmatic, 'rational' reassessment and reconfiguration of how individuals and societies perceive of themselves as mutually-suffering subjects in a world we cannot fully comprehend. His philosophy, in this context, is a radical break with the common-sense logic of his time, with the -theisms and philosophical mainstream that governed his world and with the bourgeoning political and economic complex that sought to alienate people from one another and to control and limit their possibility. But by stating fundamentally that we're all the same — suffering, dejected, meaningless beings — Schopenhauer's philosophy is a call to arms for an imaginative naysaying to the rules and structural meaning governing and steering daily life and oppressing people. By proposing a fundamental denunciation of the logical/affirmationist basis by which authority clings to its power (be it moral, political or religious authority), Schopenhauer's view is a pure critique of reason and authority on a cosmic scale that takes aim against authority for its incapacity to make better of the cursed situation that befalls each existing, suffering subject.

Georg Lukacs, like many other more practically minded Marxists, whilst recognising a value in a thorough denial and denunciation of authority and the structuring, governing logic that plagues mankind, denounces Schopenhauer for his apparent defeatism, schadenfreude and revelling (intellectually, at least) in suffering.[20] Here we can surely agree Lukacs is being a little reductionist and binary, and it is perhaps more accurate that Schopenhauer's 'pleasure' is, in fact, taken in the speculative pursuit of and philosophical diagnosis of the suffering inherent in existence (not to mention his call to aestheticism as a pleasure begetting a certain freedom of mind from the world). Again, less misanthropy and more pleasure in his own anti-establishment intellectual innovations and ability to antagonise his contemporaries. For Lukacs (though argued much more eruditely), philosophy is nothing unless it sparks a connection between theory and praxis, otherwise it is just an ascetic exercise of metaphysical masturbation; and, as Marx argues, philosophy exists to change the world. For Schopenhauer, however, philosophy exists to demonstrate the futility of change in the world — nonetheless, a change in perception and relationship with the world remains possible. Philosophy exists not in a materialist sense to provoke a change in the world's formation and conditions (hence the pessimism), but to change the fundamental way in which the world is thought of and experienced. Ultimately, if Marxism adds to the world, Schopenhauer's philosophy seeks to reduce the world to nought, to a pure negation.

The question we should then ask is not whether pessimism undermines Marxism or whether a pessimistic outlook necessarily negates radicalism or not. For Eugene Thacker, Schopenhauer's pessimism is a response to the abandonment of the principle of 'sufficient reason', a radical statement of antagonism that ultimately stimulates and postulates the necessity (irrespective of the underlying scepticism towards this possibility) of an alternative. But to what extent can pessimism, a speculative anti-establishment discourse, be thought of in a practicable way toward socio-cultural or political change? Perhaps it is here that we may propose a dispensing (or retooling) of fundamental metaphysical Schopenhauerisms and begin to run his thought experiments through a more specific grounding, to think conceptually of the world as the negative aggregate of not simply this nexus, cosmic 'Will', but of the 'Will *of Capital*' — or perhaps even more fancifully, 'the Will to life *of Capital*' — and pessimism as diagnostic of and a response to this. And while Schopenhauer bemoans existence in which there exists no redemption, he does maintain there is a need to pursue and practice compassion to some degree. A hope of sorts? A compassion that is the self-recognising and identifying with the suffering other. A self that recognises the shared experience of suffering and in so doing comes to see themself not as 'I in my world' but 'I, as part of a world that is against us'.

To provocatively surmise what has been postulated thus far, we can say that existence, according to Schopenhauer at least, is the absolute negative. Irredeemable. Unknowable. But to begin to move this equation into a territory that at least begs the question of a response, requires some speculative utopian thinking. To add nothing to '*existence* = *absolute negative*', to simply 'be', to facilitate continuity equates to existence as continued and never-ending absolute negative. Conversely, to act in a positive way — that is, to 'add' something tangible, something accountable — still cannot outweigh the absolute weight of negativity. Absolute, intangible negativity, plus tangible, accountable positive(-ism), equates to a negative. Negative infinity plus two is still a pretty one-sided affair. However, when absolute negative (existence) meets absolute (intangible) *positive*, and by this we of course mean a countering impossibility, a negation of the negative — a utopia — conceived here as absolute negativity *without* the negativity, the remainder is dead zero. Nothingness, the best of all possible outcomes — and the pessimist at the back heckles a sardonic 'I told you so...'.

In this context, the value of pessimism as a critical device is found in the consciousness-raising assertion that perhaps there is no escape, no exit — or at least, no relief to be found in the abandonment of self or the world — and, as such, a new imaginative conception must be thought of. Though our utopias may be as doomed as our reality/realities, it is not to say an ecstatic or antagonistic pleasure cannot be found in the imagination of this other which counters that which is so detested in the current state of affairs. This task was one which Walter Benjamin wrote passionately about in his famous essay on surrealism, wherein he identifies and lauds the surrealists for their ability to cast 'profane illumination' on the world through their art and for their ecstatic engagement with revolution in all its forms. In so doing, Benjamin's eschatological answer calls upon us, as the surrealists did, to 'mistrust in the fate of freedom, mistrust in the fate of [...] humanity, but three times mistrust in all reconciliation'.[21]

More provocative than most, the controversial British philosopher Nick Land argues that 'Pessimism is the first truly transcendental critique, operating against being'. In his highly complex and inflammatory analysis and critique of contemporary philosophy and culture, *Thirst for Annihilation: Georges Bataille and Virulent Nihilism* (1992), Land identifies two distinctive models for a radical stance against the bleak present. In the first instance, he cites the speculative revolutionary model which is premised on a 'taking over' of society, culture, systems and so forth. The 'overthrow of oppression-as-confinement' is a noble goal indeed; however, this process proves untenable and doomed to failure. Land's dismissal of this model comes from a cynicism that sees that the so-desired change is very much bound up in the very same processes and thinking of the present situation. His intense and performative contrarianism stems from a recognition — and perhaps acceptance — that the absurd and revolting thing cannot ultimately be changed for the better, that there is no redeeming an intrinsically bad thing. Instead, the choice becomes one between the accelerating of its worst excesses to the point at which it breaks (or the subject finds a perverse satisfaction in being the revolting thing) or to retreat or withdraw entirely to negate its most detrimental effects. In essence, this is a pessimistic choice: One challenges or changes a thing or power by *becoming* the thing or power, or one adopts the second model premised on 'escape' — either way, there is no happy-living with it, only a sardonic and spiteful naysaying.[22]

Nick Land is curious in that his writings of the 1990s, particularly, often gravitate between this kind of pessimism and nihilism, in that he reports on life as a grievous mistake and a fundamentally meaningless absurdity, but he also seems to advocate an annihilating journey through capitalism/Western philosophical and political orthodoxy as the basis for a deeply unsettling neo-reactionary and posthuman, or anti-human, utopian turn. As McKenzie Wark states, Land 'did not shy away from the horrors of techno-capitalism' and indeed devotes much of his exhilaratingly schizophrenic corpus of writings to addressing the implications and conditions of a techno-capitalism (apparently far more advanced and frightening than the 'proto-capitalism' to which socialism is concerned with) in which information, as a vitalising commodity, becomes the capital of the twenty-first century.[23] Land's nihilism is here evident, as he sees no escape or turning from this. Indeed, his *solution* is to accelerate the process, to get it over and done with! 'Machinic pragmatism'.[24] Land's expression of this in his writing can and does make the Marxist shudder as, channelling

Lyotard's provocative and oft-derided *Libidinal Economy*, he aligns the death drive and labour (which is now found in strictly virtual and cognitive pursuits aligned with digital culture and techno-capitalism) with a necessary (re-)vitalisation/annihilation of the subject. In short, he sees the advancement of technology into the processes of labour as something that, firstly, changes the human being and accelerates their intersection into techno-capitalism (and by extension annihilation); and secondly, is something we actually unconsciously desire, as it leads towards to a solution of sorts from the impasse of increasingly demeaning and meaningless labour — some kind of breakthrough towards a virtual materialism; think of the Nietzschean *Übermensch* in the form of the *Cognio-Machina*, an Artificial Intelligence in its purest sense. There is undoubtably a euphoric tone exhorted in Land's critique that seems to welcome the impending collapse and meltdown of all contingent society into a 'pure' capitalism.

Land's contrarianism is, however, symptomatic of a wider distrust of a cultural and philosophical agenda that promotes optimistic and genial approaches. It is both ironic and deeply concerning that this sense of pessimistic incredulity has been violently adopted into the neo-reactionary rhetoric of right-wing and far-right political movements in their accelerated denial and condemnation of human rights, equality, economic/sexual/social freedoms, etc. rather than by the Left, who have arguably failed to adequately or practically mobilise their base's frustration, concern and anger with the same level of vitality against the increasing obfuscation, denial and roll-back of these essential values.

So far, this all sounds like unabashed negativism of the worst kind, a dark cloud on everyone's day, that does not actually get us much closer to telling us anything new about how to overcome or retool society, culture or existence, nor help us work out a way through our human predicament. Benjamin Noys argues that the Left must adopt a stance that actively engages with the negative and does not shy away from the inherent contradictions and failures of an optimistic consensus in philosophical and political approaches to radicalism. Whilst negativity is often caricatured as the glorification of nihilistic abstractions over practicable solutions, with little regard for or a thoroughgoing denial of our present reality, the return to negativity, for Noys, allows an 'immanent traversal' of the most pressing and horrific abstraction, that of capitalist values and ontology.[25] As Noys articulates:

> capital itself is a kind of pure relationality, a pure abstraction of value, labour, and accumulation, which can only be 'seen' in negative. This is why the negation of real abstractions demands further abstraction, as abstraction is the only possible means to reveal this.[26]

Negativity, here, is valid as a speculative, critical tool that allows for a thoroughgoing exposition and dismantling of ontological positions and pretentions. Absolute negation, the rejection and refusal of a given, whether individually or collectively, stimulates the breakdown of the entire ontological scaffold supporting the neoliberal capitalist reality and capitalist realism.

Concurrent with this notion, the moral recuperation of pessimistic naysaying to the world is increasingly being brought to the fore. Crucially, it is emerging in direct refutation of the overbearing triumphalism of many on the political right, emboldened by a wave of writers, critics and cultural commentators who, in their blinkered insistence on progressivism and tracing of human 'progress', serve only to further certify and justify deeply entrenched conservative-capitalist values such as laissez-faire economics and further vindicate Western enlightenment values. As a critical and aesthetic tool, pessimism is increasingly being used to explore the meaninglessness of reality, the abhorrence or evil inherent in the world (or systems that shape the world), the instability of meaning and its mutation/appropriation by various political and cultural malefactors and, lastly, the apparent nightmare of consciousness or experience within *this version* of the world. In recent years, from both an existential and political standpoint or application, openly pessimistic thought has garnered much more of a critical purchase and has been the subject of several noteworthy studies by critics who have sought to answer — or at least consider — some of these emergent questions which countenance the abandonment of the optimistic position, diagnose the underlying tragedy of existence and speculate on possible ways of navigating this in the social, cultural and political arena.

In her excellent *Dark Matters: Pessimism and the Problem of Suffering* (2021), Mara van der Lugt presents pessimism as being fundamentally concerned with speaking 'truthfully, meaningfully and compassionately about suffering'. Pessimism, in this framework, is a discourse of absolute moral orientation and significance that forces a subject to consider not only the cause and nature of suffering but to (re)consider one's own commitment to lessening that suffering in the world.[27] Joshua Foa Dienstag's *Pessimism: Philosophy, Ethic, Spirit* (2009), approaches the subject of pessimism from an altogether different, though crucially insightful, angle.[28] Less concerned with superficial pursuits in metaphysical conjecture and existential and moral wrangling — or the nexus question of evil, which all boils down to a judgement as to life's fundamental worth or value — Dienstag's concern is in the practical and political application of pessimism. Dienstag reads pessimism as a stimulus to political action and change, and while the pessimist expects nothing, the ethical pessimist is spurred on from their position of desolation and discontent to rebel and take necessary action against the perceived causes of their ire. Far from being a rather passé question of whether life is worth living or not, then, pessimism is a vibrant (though somewhat dimly lit) and highly charged critical discourse, and despite many popular misgivings, a sign of intellectual maturity, radical political engagement and a thoroughly moral position.

As we turn, at this point, to the idea of utopia, it is worth us stopping a moment to question, ethically, existentially and politically, what it is that pessimism demands. Is it a radical break or negation of the existent hegemon? The promotion or striving for a universal level of tolerable or acceptable negativism for everyone as possibly the best most realistic and possible outcome for all concerned? Nothingness — or the cold, encompassing embrace of the void? Or does pessimism demand nothing at all, but instead benevolently offer a black mirror to the now: an incursion like a quiet stain of possibility against the positivist sheen of contemporary discourse and rationality? In what follows, I will propose a speculative redirection of negativism into the utopian model as a means to address the existential despair of our lives, or more specifically, of lives lived in our *particular* kind of despair that is attributable to hegemonic capitalism of our present moment. But before doing so, it is important to now turn to the question of utopia and utopianism as a 'hopeful pessimism and form of potential radical, eschatological discourse or alternative'.

3. A NOTE ON UTOPIA

The critical recuperation of pessimism has a value in a very specific pursuit of a utopian, anti-capitalist alternative. As such, we must now turn our attention towards the utopian dream of alterity itself. In so doing, we may extrapolate and raise some of the moral, ethical, political and existential questions that continue to influence and provoke modern conceptualisations of utopia, particularly within the context of socio-cultural systems of power, politics and the global hegemony of neoliberal capitalist absolutism.

The concept of utopia has been a staple of Eastern and Western philosophical and political discourse for as long as humans have been telling each other stories about good places and bad ones. The term utopia, as commonly understood today and deriving from the Greek word for 'no place', however, was coined by Thomas More, in the sixteenth century in his satirical book *De optimo rei publicae statu deque nova insula Utopia*, or more simply, *Utopia*. The narrative itself describes the fictional island society of Utopia, where rationality and science govern and a great spirit of equality, communalism and community, rather than an elitist or hierarchical order, is fostered. Further still, Utopia is a land wherein those living there are generally happy and prosperous, where greed and immorality are scarce and crime and war virtually non-existent. In the context of sixteenth century Europe, to which his work responded, such lofty goals were indeed the stuff of radical and almost treasonous fictitious speculation.

More recently (relatively speaking), since the nineteenth century, and arguably since the publication of Marx and Engels' *The Communist Manifesto* in 1848, the idea of a Marxist utopia has inspired and frustrated philosophical, cultural and political debate. In this utopian vision, the demand is for a world free from the shackles and prison of capital and class: extract society and the individual from a repressive capitalist system — or eradicate that system entirely — and humanity becomes, in a sense, free to experience life in its full joy. However, there has always remained the burning question as to what happens when this utopian change is made — when we do become 'untethered', so to speak. This is a question posed by Jordan Peele's 2019 horror film *Us*, wherein an abandoned multitude of subterranean doppelgangers are led, through a violent retributive revolution, to collectively overturn the systemic hierarchy and governmental conspiracy that had kept them down and dehumanised, exploited and oppressed, whilst those aboveground have thrived.[29] When they do take over, and at the end of the film, their hands are clasped together, making a human chain across America, symbolic of their power and potential. Akin to how the 2005 film *V for Vendetta* ends, revolutionary utopian potential is glancingly eluded to but not fully envisioned or materialised.[30] In his crass and oft-repeated response to the ending of the latter, Slavoj Žižek retorts that he would quite happily sell his grandmother into slavery for a *V for Vendetta, Part 2,* so that he could witness the aftermath of the takeover, how the revolutionary multitude would organise and actualise their utopian goals in the real world, beginning the day after. Whilst I would not offer my grandmother quite so freely, I would be intrigued to see what would have happened next in *Us, Part 2,* after the uprising. How would the untethered organise their society and life above ground? Would they, having suffered tremendously, embark on a radical project and counter hierarchical system fostered on the principles of compassion and an understanding of a shared trauma within and subject to an exploitative hegemon? Their hands across America, symbolising, not just their reach and power, but their own recognition that their power is relative only to their connection as equals to one another. Or, after the killing, would they just stand in a field not knowing what to do with themselves until deciding to fall into the places and lives of their murdered counterparts? A tethering of sorts (again) to the system and structure of the reality they inhabit, for their failure to articulate and enact any kind of alternative. Deep down, the pessimist perhaps already knows the most likely outcome of this story.

J.G. Ballard's novel, *Super-Cannes* (2000), poses an excellent further opportunity to explore the fraught concept of utopia within the contemporary, or late-capitalist, Western imagination and precisely exhibits a vision counter to the Marxist utopia hitherto alluded to.[31] The novel itself centres on the dilemmas and descent of protagonist Paul Sinclair, resident of the prestigious new Eden-Olympia complex. Eden-Olympia presents itself as the embodiment of the utopian modern society in which fantasy meets reality, work meets play, and obscene wealth meets obscene desire. Built of glass and titanium, clad in ventilation shafts and electrical cables, and situated directly under the sweltering sun, aside the picturesque French-Mediterranean coastline, Eden-Olympia, to the reader, resembles a glistening yet abrasive, promethean yet anti-human monument to man's achievements and possibilities within the boundaries of capitalism. Described as a masterpiece of modern rationality, Eden-Olympia maximises social conditioning and facilitates the dispensing of morality to ensure that the corporate executives and workers that call this place 'home' can focus intently on the fulfilment of their potential through work.

It is a world constructed as the perfect embodiment of human ambition and opulence, simultaneously and meticulously refined as a peerless hub of hyper-productivity: an environment built specifically to deliver what Marx described as the 'abstraction of the worker' and the transformation of 'living labour into a mere living accessory of this machinery'.[32] Here we are presented with an inversion of the Marxist argument that labour and capital are barriers to freedom, as the utopianism of the development is founded on the principle of hard work, exclusivity and wealth. A futuristic wonderland obfuscating reality. A beacon to human progressivism and a veritable utopia of a particular, accelerationist, capitalist sort, whereby every enhancement has been made to ensure a subject's fidelity to the park's ontology. The park as the artificial embodiment of the most excessive privileges of capitalist psychopathology: *jouissance* without compromise, excess without morals, capitalism without limits. Paul, however, is something of an outlier amongst the park's residents. A former editor and critic, he is soon bored by its soullessness and imposing artificiality and becomes obsessed with trying to uncover the obscene underside to this utopia that seems to exist beyond the carefully stage-managed and polished façade. In so doing, Paul's quest for meaning, logic and — above all — order, stemming from an inherent mistrust of the capitalist regime, comes face to face with a troubling, malignant psychology that thrives and drives the otherwise glistening utopian model for an enhanced capitalist twenty-first century.

Super-Cannes, much like Ballard's later novels, including *Cocaine Nights*, *Millennium People* and *Kingdom Come*, is committed to exploring worlds or societies, communes and groups wherein their desire for absolute freedom (most prominently typified by the desire for violence, perversion and excess) assumes a greater precedence and nascency in the hyper-capitalist or utopian-capitalist playgrounds of contemporary society here so accurately imagined. Within *Super-Cannes*, the utopian fantasies of a world of pure freedom without limits are authorised and legitimised — and indeed encouraged, facilitated and manipulated — by systemic forces of authority that desire ever-higher functioning and emotionally and ideologically invested subjects of control. Whilst *Super-Cannes* is ostensibly a parodic critique of the ways in which neoliberalism invests itself into the psychology of the subject, it is telling that the author cannot fully and completely disregard the 'psychopathology' of his characters/communities. *Super-Cannes* subverts neoliberalism in its critique, but simultaneously and disturbingly, the representation of Eden-Olympia's success reveals the strength of neoliberalism's hold on contemporary society and politics as a supposed utopian model. As resistance fails in the novel, and no tangible vision beyond the accelerated capitalism and politics of Eden-Olympia are revealed, it becomes evident that ideology has co-opted and subsumed utopianism. In the capitalist-utopia, individuals are stripped of all human moral impulse, and their motivating desire, their 'will to life', so to speak, becomes transposed into the process of capitalism itself. Here, utopia and the hyper-extension of neoliberal ideology are one and the same.

It is for this reason that some argue that, ultimately, Marxism does not go far enough. The overturning of capitalism (irrespective of whether it is a *utopian removal of Capitalism* or *the removal of Utopian-Capitalism*) isn't enough to 'save' the world if we've been stripped of our capacity to think completely and alternatively. Both actions, toward utopia or the unwinding of the capitalist-utopian system, after the initial ecstatic moment (we can, of course, afford ourselves, at least, that scant moment of relief and victory), necessitate a carefully planned actualisation of a system to follow which does not repeat the failures of history (The Paris Commune or Soviet-era Communism, for example) or degenerate into or reveal itself as another version of the very thing it is ostensibly opposed to.

This bind and sense of disillusionment, in the past decade or two particularly, has been further propagated by 'accelerationism' as an ultimately utopian, or radical leftist model of resistance:

> Acceleration is a political heresy: the insistence that the only
> radical political response to capitalism is not to protest,
> disrupt, or critique, nor to await its demise at the hands
> of its own contradictions, but to accelerate its uprooting,
> alienating, decoding, abstractive tendencies.[33]

Emerging from French post-structuralist thought in the 1970s, the thought experiment proposed that if no alternative is imaginable, nor practicable, then a reinvestment of desire and energy into its systems and practices may be necessary to extract some modicum of value. Deleuze and Guattari proposed the need to accelerate the processes of production, not to withdraw from its processes, but to go further still. Most famous in this regard was Lyotard's controversial provocation that the worker experiences a masochistic pleasure in the imposed destruction of their body through work. To paraphrase his controversial claim in *Libidinal Economy* (1974), yes, we suffer through capitalism, but this does not also mean we cannot enjoy this suffering.[34] It is a provocation central to Ballard's novel, one which Wilder Penrose, Eden-Olympia's resident psychologist and arch-architect of the park's inherent pathology, advocates and facilitates in his patients in pursuit of his perfect society. Indeed, the accelerationist trend of criticism as a discussion of an ontology of utopia, over the past decade in particular, increasingly becomes a tautological exercise in reimagined capitalist progressivism and idealism.

What is curious and revealing in the novel is that, despite the violence, the perversion and the sadism accepted by the park's residents, it is optimism that thrives — optimism that these are necessary evils in the pursuit of communal and societal perfectibility. The residents are in this sense pioneers on the path towards societal improvement brought forth by the advancement of neoliberal principles, or as Penrose surmises: 'A giant multinational like Fuji or General Motors sets its own morality. The company defines the rules that govern ... We can rely on their judgment, and that leaves us free to get on with the rest of our lives'.[35] For Wilder Penrose, violence and transgression in this context are rehabilitative energies in the continuation of his utopian vision of an exclusive society wherein subjects are assets and conduits toward the perfectibility of a neoliberal capitalist agenda. Rather than a spontaneous, creative eruption that challenges the inherent contradictions of the park's ontology and subverts structures of power, here they become the obscene economy that the park lives off.

That the business park/accelerationist utopia in *Super-Cannes* manages to reinvest 'freedoms', particularly those enlivened through transgression, and turn them into something productive (or at least profitable) echoes the concern of many critics and commentators of postmodernism and modern capitalism: that what we typically think of as being resistant to or antagonistic towards capitalism is in fact little threat at all. And this is the central, terrifying conceit: the ideology and ontology of capitalism has consumed even the imagined possibility of its own downfall. To this end, the 'logic' or ideology of capitalism becomes the mediator of its own alternative or other. We cannot conceivably discern of 'utopia' (in the anti-capitalist sense) except by the very terms of the thing we need it to counter, which, counter-intuitively, further cements the pre-eminence of the undesirable thing itself. The question then becomes how to re-enthuse a pragmatic response against this? Moreover, how to even speculate towards any kind of utopian alternative at all that is not simply repackaged capitalist-utopian-progressivism?

Perhaps a slight adjustment of how we view the concept of utopia is necessary? Rather than tying the notion to optimistic gestures of imagination (which we have vilified enough in this chapter), let us consider instead that utopias are borne of a pessimistic disaffirmation of reality. Utopias, in this reconfiguration, bear a negation of values based on the fundamental premise that our belief and investment in systems of political and social order are baseless fallacies. Particularly evident is an increased desire or fantasy to explore existence(s) — utopian alternatives — characterised by a transvaluation of cultural and political limits and values that can be said to fall somewhere between the Schopenhauerian rejection of idealistic and illusionary phenomenalism and the Nietzschean critical diagnosis of life's ubiquitous tragedy, and later, the affirmation of existence through nihilism and the rejection of paradigm values.

Paul Ricoeur, the twentieth-century French philosopher who spent the greater part of his career examining the phenomenology of hermeneutics (or the experience of understanding), examined the conflict existing between the concept of utopia and the ideology against which it responds. Utopia, he argued, is ultimately an imagined world that exists beyond ideology, which, in Ricoeur's estimation, relates to the specifically socio-political and cultural forms or ideas that hold society and societies within a particular power structure or modality of control.[36] When reality becomes unpalatable, when the ideological foundations of a ruinous existent system are unveiled, utopias can offer the subject the opportunity to imagine an alternative: to idealise an alternate or other world that plays to a different tune. There is, of course, a paradox here in that by their very nature, utopias exist in no-place — beyond reality — and, as such, the conception of utopia is followed by a return to dependence on ideology and the disappointing reality one sought to escape in one's utopian flight of fancy. Utopia cannot exist in actuality; by contrast, ideology — or the ideas that inform the structure of power and control — seems even more inescapable and binding. For Ricoeur, politics exist specifically to mediate between the two; it is the praxis by which these two contrary ideas, ideology and utopianism, are conceptualised and actualised. By this logic, it becomes evident that politics and the foundations of societies are, then, borne of a disappointing compromise between control and freedom: a few degrees too warm for the idealogues and a few degrees too cold for the utopians, resulting ultimately in a hopeless bind where everyone remains somewhat uncomfortable, muttering contempt and derision at the temperature of the room.

While Ricoeur sees ideology and utopia as distinct but entwined, there are others — such as the prolific American philosopher of 'Postmodernism' fame, Fredric Jameson — who deviate, arguing that utopia is entirely bound in the ideological, rather than polar to it, and exists or functions to provoke critical negativity. Somewhat provocatively, for Jameson the best utopias are, in fact, those which fail, and the failure of the utopian ideal is, in his estimation, a necessity of a healthy functioning critical intellect and the persistence of the ability to challenge power. Utopian visions and ideas are better understood, in this regard, as fundamental to the process of unveiling the inherent negativism within the ideological fabric of the present and responding to this with imagination and bravery. That is, with the bravery to sow the 'seeds of imagination' from which an *other* world or system could emerge.[37] Stripped back to its nucleus, 'utopia' is that impulse or inclination toward an escape or alternative, predicated at the point when, seeing the world or system (or an element, function or component of this) critically, we reject it. Only when the world/system is unveiled, and the horrors it incites, the pernicious nature of its mechanics and the malign codes underpinning its very fabric are laid bare, does 'utopia' emerge as a critical negation of the existent. In this sense, utopia is a fantasy and escapism, which is to a certain extent fine. The worth of a critical tool is not always (nor should it necessarily be) measured by the tangible strength of its praxis, by its 'doing', but also by the sense of possibility and the emotive and rebellious energies that it may provoke on a subjective and collective or phenomenological level.

In his essay 'The Limits of Utopia', the British novelist, essayist and critic China Miéville argues that at the precipice of ecological collapse and societal catastrophe, utopia — an alternative world, a changed world, a better world — is needed.[38] And yet, like a malign and despicable joke, the impulses and ideals needed for rethinking change are co-opted into the system and logic of capitalism itself. To this end, utopia can also be a pernicious and deadly concept, particularly on the subject of the environment. Fredric Jameson posits that the story of capitalism has essentially been about a series of land grabs. While we can take issue with this particular notion (particularly in a more digital, deterritorialised world wherein data, intellect/ideas and information are increasingly sought as the capital of the twenty-first century), this general idea does hold merit and is notable throughout Miéville's polemic essay, which describes how environmentalist issues (and quite often the literal utopian attempts to save and recover the planet) have become big business and the realm of global capitalist forces.

On utopia, Miéville, writes:

Utopianism isn't hope, still less optimism: it is need, and it is desire. For recognition, like all desire, and/but for the specifics of its reveries and programmes, too; and above all for betterness *tout court*. For alterity, something other than the exhausting social lie. For rest. And when the cracks in history open wide enough, the impulse may even jimmy them a little wider.[39]

It is important that we expand on this distinction. Utopianism, as Miéville contends, is desire for alterity or alternative specifically from wider social life as we live and understand it. But further still, utopianism is the instinct to act, to antagonise, to press against the weight of history and systems of power. If utopianism is the desire for a thing, utopia is the fetishised, imaginary, impossible thing that allows for such tensions and contestations to be examined. A sandbox of revolutionary and anti-establishment potential. As a rallying call to the hope for a better world, the need for collective utopian framework or idea is clear. Nonetheless, 'Utopia!' alone is as insufficient as a cooling balm lightly applied to a raging third-degree burn. Utopia (in the singular, concrete sense, as opposed to utopia as an unfixed concept, as multiplicitous and unrestricted possibility) can stymie invention, radicalism and change and, worse still, can help to shape and give form to the detested ideology of globalised, neoliberal capitalism itself. Contorted by the hand of capitalism, even the task (or impossible dream, given how far past redeemability it would seem we are as a species on this planet) of improving the environment, reducing carbon emissions and weaning ourselves off the habits of production and consumption that are destroying the world cannot now be untied from capitalism's logic of profit, accumulation and destruction. That is why, as Miéville describes it, the world's wealthy can offset their carbon emissions by funding technologies and projects that seek to depollute the atmosphere, or to create ecotopias — vast spaces of freshly planted trees and preserves for nature's due benefit. In reality, this often involves large corporations, in cahoots with bought governments, disposing of their toxic waste on someone else's doorstep — of course, typically the poor or the marginalised communities of the world — or reclaiming swathes of land for ecological projects; by which I, of course, mean brutally disposessing people of their lands and homes — again, of course, typically the poor or marginalised communities of the world. Always, with capitalism, accumulation and creation necessitates a dispossession and destruction. It is one of the great clichés of our time that it is now easier to imagine the end of the world than the end of capitalism. In Miéville's critique of utopia, particularly in the context of environmental challenges and the idealism that underpins massive scientific endeavours to 'hack' the planet, through geoengineering and such, to roll back the destruction wrought on the Earth, it become easier and more palatable for us to 'imagine the deliberate transformation of the entire planet than of our political economy'.[40] Grand endeavours that might be celebrated as triumphs of human exceptionalism in the face of catastrophic ecological collapse are in fact the capitulation of the radical imagination, the 'surrender to the status quo' and the 'exoneration of entrenched power'.[41]

It is partly for this reason why Fredric Jameson is happy to contend that utopianism is not necessarily concerned with the finished product, nor with defence or invention of specifics, 'but rather the story of all the arguments about how Utopia should be constructed in the first place'.[42] Less the practicalities, more the energies, the possibilities and the examination of the intellect that is provoked and spurred on by recognition, disaffection and disputation. In a contemporary capitalist society that increasingly colonises the mind and construes a common-sense logic based on the primacy of its own values, the ability to imagine the impossible, to process and produce any kind of framework is to be lauded. This is precisely Jameson's point in his controversial manifesto for a contemporary, utopian society founded on the creation of a socialist-leaning universal army wielding altruistic power over a society, which is subsequently unshackled from the binds of class antagonism and the labour-wage bind. In *An American Utopia*,

Jameson provocatively argues that revolution itself — rather than the perfect society beyond — is the utopian goal. Impossible, by the logic of the global capitalist hegemony, but a necessary and crucial pursuit towards a power shift nonetheless. Therein, however, lies a fundamental problem. Fully aware of this disjunction, Jameson's manifesto shows that whilst previously heralded as the political programme of the Left, revolution more presently has all but disappeared as a viable utopian project — in part because of a lack of agency and belief in the outcome of revolution and, simultaneously, in part because of the overwhelming omnipresence and reach of the very system that revolution sought to displace. While utopianism has always been concerned with systems of power and exposing their flaws and insufficiencies, it seems that the notion of utopia itself has fallen prey to these very systems. To labour a point, capitalism's success has been to imbue and invest itself so heavily in all aspects of life that an alternative become unimaginable, impossible. As we've previously illustrated through our brief interlude on Ballard's novel, utopia is often co-opted into the rhetoric and ideological function of the capitalist system, diminished as a radical pursuit and transformed as the rally call of those preaching the virtues of neoliberal capitalism and conservatism in the twenty-first century. Jameson's intervention, however, despite being somewhat impractical, historically tone-deaf and purposefully incendiary, does succeed in its incitement of a critical and imaginary reconsideration of revolutionary utopianism, which the Left may benefit from exploring — at least in spirit, if not imitation.

If we accept that the wanton idealism of optimism is baseless and irrational, an alternative must be sought. Pessimism, at the very least, is premised on a necessary assessment that things are not perfect, and there is of course no sound basis to believe they ever will be if we maintain our current trajectory. Pessimism, as discussed, is thus a vital component of utopian radicalism. As Miéville concurs, 'activism without the pessimism that rigor should provoke is just sentimentality', and further still, 'utopia without rage and fury is indulgence'.[43] To push this further, I contend that what unites both pessimism and utopianism is a shared concern or, further still, a vitally important underlying engagement with negativism. Benjamin Noys, in *The Persistence of the Negative*, argued that 'only through the reconfiguration of negativity as a practice [...] can we develop more supple and precise forms of resistance and struggle within and against capitalism'.[44] In this manner, utopia becomes the engendered negation — the reconception of a thing without that which had been terrifyingly and bleakly discerned by the pessimist's lament against the thing in its current entirety: the twenty-first century *without* capitalism; society *without* inequality; economy *without* work; labour *without* toil; life *without* suffering; the world *without* us. Pessimism and utopianism are engaged in a reciprocal relationship based on their inherent critique, disavowal and ultimate desire to negate, escape or prompt a radical break from a subjective and collective state of disjunction or disappointment. Pessimism is ultimately, then, for the disconsolate participant/critic of the contemporary, the diagnosis prompting the (speculative) utopian curative dream.

4. DISCONSOLATE DREAMERS

Beginning at a point of resignation that considers the socio-political and cultural horizons of twenty-first-century capitalism almost unsurmountable (particularly in the wake and failure of current existing 'alternatives'), and that there is little by way of a tangible or credible redeeming arc for humanity to cling to, in these final notes, I speculate a path towards a radical, utopian escape. An alternative of sorts, which is premised on a particularly existential violence against — or abandonment of — the self-as-conduit of capitalism and the reconceptualisation of the possibility of the negative, which, aesthetically and intellectually, has the capacity to provoke a utopian break or disentanglement from the darkness of the present and our binds to neoliberal capitalism.

In Thomas Ligotti's hauntingly evocative short story 'The Town Manager', a sense of abject hopelessness or resignation permeates that only serves to confirm the need for a pragmatic, pessimistic response. In this narrative, the reader follows the protagonist and his fellow townsfolk through a series of transitions from one government leader to another, culminating with a town manager who belligerently scribbles his demands for nonsensical or ill-intentioned policies without challenge or recrimination whilst ruling with absolute tyranny over a disempowered and exploited citizenry who, 'nonetheless, still had to go through the motions'.[45] For the townsfolk, this grim state of affairs is simply

[t]he order of things into which [they] had been born and to which [they] had committed [themselves] by compliance. The risk of opposing this order, of plunging into the unknown, was simply too much to contemplate for very long.[46]

It is a story that functions as a parable of the absurd and mendacious nature society at large, as it is coerced and compelled by political forces motivated by greed and self-interest to act in ways that are detrimental to the communal good. Here, the new town manager comes in and immediately sets about ordering his subjects to transform the town into a sideshow attraction — 'Funny Town' — and then, once the attraction lost its appeal, disappears with every penny of revenue generated.

In 'The Town Manager', characters are systematically trapped within, and violently constrained by, forces beyond their understanding. Specifically, here, they are trapped by a fear of change and loyalty to traditional lore. In this narrative, though, life for the town's population becomes a routine of the grotesquely absurd. As the narrator exhorts, 'those of us who lived [in the town] functioned as sideshow freaks', puppets and slaves to the unknown malefactor as their abhorrent vision for the society is put into practice.[47] As such, this story functions as a pejorative retort to those who hold any lingering optimistic faith in government acting in ways that foster the dignity and well-being of its people.

When the narrator finally becomes overwhelmed with disillusionment at the absurdity and ridiculousness of the town's machinations, he decides to disentangle himself and to walk away from it all. This act is one borne of dejection and disconsolation but also enabled by a utopian hope and belief that elsewhere must exist something better. However, as is consistent with Ligotti's wider literary intention to rain copious amounts of misery and punishment on anyone with even the vaguest temerity to expect better, the narrator's venture is doomed to fail. 'I had fled that place', he admits:

> I passed through many towns, as well as large cities, doing clean-up work and odd jobs to keep myself going. All of them were managed according to the same principles as my old home town, although I came upon none that had reached such an advanced stage of degeneracy. I had fled that place in hopes of finding another that had been founded upon different principles and operated under a different order. But there was no such place, or none that I could find. It seemed the only course of action left to me was to make an end of it.[48]

Conventional life, as a participant citizen of the town, is the adversary which the narrator must overcome, either through acceptance or through a somewhat self-destructive resignation and disavowal of the certainties of their reality. At the end of the story, for the narrator at least, negation from this world (no matter the cost) is preferable. Strangely, it is at this point of pessimistic confirmation that an alternative is presented. Conversely, this alternative is an escape further *into* the system, in the form of a career in town management.

Here, rather than some kind of positivist approach to overturn a detrimental government or culture, the protagonist feels further compelled to grind out his existence and to meander on in a state of ironic acceptance. In so doing, rather than attempting to make an end of it, the narrator edges towards another 'solution' of sorts. In this post-hope world, he is unable to overcome an inherently bad thing. Instead, he subscribes to a survival premised on *becoming* the inherently bad thing — by taking up a career in town management. His response is a sign of resignation and ironic acceptance towards a present state of affairs that renders life as beyond any positivist reprieve or alternative. At the story's conclusion, then, hopelessness belies a cynical, somewhat self-destructive pragmatism reflected in the abandonment of self, principle, confidence and expectation.

Resignation, as Ligotti's short story exemplifies, is an enticing, though problematic, notion in the conceptualisation of a utopian escape. Though while this story ultimately concludes with a resigned fall back into the system, resignation (whether as a refusal to participate, a cynical disengagement, a negation or refusal, or as self-effacing act) can be a powerful eschatological and political motif in the twenty-first century. As examined in what follows, resignation, which is tantamount to an almost disconsolate sense of dejection with the world, leads on to questions of political and existential disengagement or disentanglement.

Italian cultural theorist, activist and philosopher Franco 'Bifo' Berardi has emerged as one of the preeminent diagnosticians for the bleak cultural predicament we, in Western societies, face in the wake of an advancing, accelerating capitalism that dominates both the materialist world and the cognitive realm. For Berardi, 'Semiocapitalism', a description borrowed from Baudrillard but developed throughout Berardi's career from around the late 1990s, reflects the extent to which capitalism has intruded into and absorbed the entirety of human existence and has rendered everything a sign or element within the logic of capitalism. In today's world, the subject is alienated from their humanity and locked into the circuit of capitalistic 'circuit of goods' that ultimately ties a subject's labour to notions of self-identity and self-realisation.[49] In this world, the individual is subject to a number of reifications, or transformations into 'things', within the capitalist code on a degenerative scale from valued individual to living labour (differentiated only by one's work ID number), to semi-sentient source of cheap data, to emotionally vacant data input conduit of system.

As Mark Fisher describes it, the present world is beset by the belief 'that there's no alternative to capitalism', and an 'attitude of resignation and fatalism in the face of this — a sense that all we can do is accommodate ourselves [...] and limit our hopes to containing its worst excesses'.[50] Fisher's seminal, *Capitalist Realism*

(2009) presented a thorough diagnostic critique of neoliberal capitalism's real-world and metaphysical application, as it supplants natural or alternative values and desires with a staged fantasy of capitalist exchange.[51] Moreover, it describes a pervasive atmosphere that is found in all areas of cultural, social and political life and corresponds with the intellectual and institutional suppression and devaluation of any form or concept of alternative to capitalism (be it rational, violent, intellectual or otherwise).

Akin to Fisher, Berardi argues that the cognitive, desiring and emotional capacities of workers are now employed and trapped within the mechanisms — or more appropriately to our digital age, the algorithmic codes, or codified realms — of capitalism; but, for Berardi, a salvaging is possible. Much of Berardi's work wrests with an attempt to navigate from resignation and despair to survive modern, post-industrial capitalism. As such, Berardi often attempts to rescue or resuscitate society's capacity to generate real value-producing knowledge, to reclaim this possibility and capacity and apply it for the greater societal good. That is, the pursuit of a communism that is not necessarily interested in the removal of work, but instead about reclaiming work as a common, shared enterprise that fosters a common good and self-realisation, rather than attending to the whims and machinations of an elitist cabal.

His response to this predicament has been vivid and consistent throughout his career, though increasingly tinged by a resignation or disconsolation and tempering of expectations. In *The Soul At Work* (2009), and with echoes of Herbert Marcuse's seminal utopian text *Eros and Civilisation* (1955), Berardi explores the ways in which humankind is subjugated under capitalism wholly and completely. For Berardi, mankind's soul — or our cognitive, emotional, aesthetic and affective components — is now captured in work: a violation far in excess of simply our bodies and time, and which renders the human subject entirely oppressed. In addition, Berardi bleakly contends that not only have we been stolen in entirety into capitalism, but the capitalist world in which we inhabit is one which has run completely amok. Ours, he argues, is a world beset by chaos, or specifically a complexity beyond understanding, which has run away from both the capacities of the human mind and capitalism itself and is the cause of an epidemic of psychological disruption that further denigrates humanity.

Berardi does not paint a particularly happy picture. We exist now within a virtual place dominated by capital that is far removed from physical space and material life and are subject to the dystopian totalitarianism of the 'logic' of capitalistic necessity.[52] In recognising the predicament wrought upon humankind, Berardi offers little to be optimistic about; indeed, his career and works throughout the late twentieth and twenty-first century reveal a lament for the failed potency of the revolutionary attempts that occupied his earlier years and an even greater lament that a universal alternative might not be materially possible anymore. Berardi is not optimistic of change, having witnessed first-hand (particularly during 1977, at the end of the Autonomia movement of mass worker revolt in his native Italy, and again, after the financial crash of 2008) how the capitalist enemy has thrived despite all resistance. Ever more so, his writing presents the future — once the preeminent utopia, 'the great empowering myth' of a temporally *new* place, that which, no matter what, we could cling to as a cause to rally around — as a possibility which has since been betrayed, lost, eaten, as we are now engulfed in our virtual world, our 'final dystopia'.[53]

Despite his often disconsolate outlook, Berardi betrays a proclivity to dream — to hope — that another possibility or alternative is even vaguely possible. A hope in the revolutionary possibility that what once was (particularly the potency of revolutionary potential of the 1970s) could emerge again. From the jaws of despair, Berardi grasps at a possibility borne of acceleration and contends that only by handing over to automation and technology can human time be freed up for more liberating activities. It is a utopian prospect Berardi readdresses in *Futurablity*, where he contends that there exists a possibility within the grasp of the worlds' knowledge workers — the so-called 'cognitariat' or the 'hacker-class', as McKenzie Wark coins them — to create something new and different. Specifically, for Berardi, it is the possibility of the liberation of human time from the constraints of labour, facilitated by the full deployment and replacement of human labour with technology: life without labour, economy without human toil, freedom without the pesky business of capitalism intruding. However, Berardi's utopia is beset by problems and challenges. Firstly, to what extent would society be comfortable with a total handover to technology and speed? If our general inability to comprehend, understand and keep up with technology is causing a psychotic rupture, as Berardi argues, then what would be the result of further committing ourselves to even more technology and speed? Secondly, Berardi's vision of happy, free human beings, left to their own devices (for the more cynical reader), resembles an evermore subaltern position, as our robotic overlords drop us into a sandbox reality while the serious and complex business of the world is left to their computational judgement. The question now would be, are we really comfortable giving greater, or ultimately total, licence to technology, information and speed, so long as they do not interfere in our more compassionate pursuits? A third concern is one which often occurs when we begin to think about alternative worlds to our own, and it becomes a question of access and the dangers of conceiving of a utopia as a closed-off space, accessible for some and not others. Berardi is right to be enthusiastic about the potential and power of the 'cognitive worker' in the twenty-first century in possessing the capacity to facilitate a real paradigm shift in the world, although it is important that we do not forget about those who do not fit this category either. While attempting to revisit Marx's binary class dialectic in a more morphogenic way befitting our digital age, Berardi inadvertently provokes another class antagonism by further dividing the working class between the 'cognitive' and 'non-cognitive' classes, when we should be trying to unite and include, not reduce or sideline.

While Berardi concedes that the likelihood of any drastic or meaningful change is slim (the 'potency' which would enable this is something which does appear limited today), this dream sustains and invigorates his radicalism and anger against the current state of the world. Possibility, he argues, can emerge from chaos, and that possibility is the nihilistic-utopian dream of a disentanglement leading to ontological freedom. Now, we can park our concerns and the practicalities of this specific project(s) for another day, but what is most important is the extent to which a negation emerges in response to despair in Berardi's conceptualisation of change and alternative — namely, the human being removed, disentangled, from system and world. 'What we need', he states, 'is not the affirmation of a will, but the disentanglement of a possibility inscribed in the present composition of the world'.[54] The possibility of which he speaks is the possibility for the cognitive capacities of a sensible-minded humankind to be untethered from the capitalist network and liberated to deploy their talents and intellect towards more compassionate and globally oriented activities.

'What can be done when nothing can be done?' Berardi mischievously askes at the end of *Heroes,* before positing his own response:

> I think that ironic autonomy is the answer. I mean the contrary of participation [...], responsibility [...], faith. Do not take part in the game, do not expect any solution from politics [...] and do not hope. Be sceptical. Do not revoke revolution.[55]

Over the past few years, and most prominently throughout the Covid-19 pandemic, participation in society, and within the economic realm particularly, has become an ever more pertinent issue. One specific trend which had emerged in recent years concerned the so-called 'Great Resignation', whereby workers had been self-directedly resigning from jobs, withdrawing themselves from the labour market (at least temporarily), at unprecedented levels in the UK and US. The extent of this refusal to work, and the unpredictability with which it struck, for a moment threatened to present an economic upheaval, with industries such as hospitality, retail, leisure and care being particularly hard hit.

Generally speaking, these kinds of sectors are notorious for preying on workers to an exploitative level, where wages are typically held quite low, zero- and short-hour contracts rife, workers are constantly told that they are easily replaceable, and the work is very often arduous. It is little surprise, then, that such workers would make the conscious decision to withdraw their labour, extricate themselves and pursue other commitments, projects or careers. But this great resignation — this evermore pervasive confidence to refuse to work — was not just limited to those in particular industries. Also particularly prominent in this were the so-called 'cognitive workers', as Berardi terms them, the digital nomads, the knowledge workers, who, untethered from their offices and released from conventional spatial-temporal ties to their employer, having been consigned to work from home, began to readdress the value of their knowledge work as a personal and social-value-producing pursuit and quickly followed the flow of labour out of the capitalist door.

Of course, there are many wholly practicable reasons why this may have occurred: the stress and difficulty of working during the pandemic; less managerial oversight when working from home meaning greater freedom in work; more free time to consider one's options; the prevalence of death and fear at the doors of humanity as a catalyst for readdressing the direction of your life and career; the opportunity to seek better remunerated work elsewhere, all feature. However, I am interested to consider that this trend (which, admittedly is now receding), as it occurred and manifested, pointed also towards — or involuntarily revealed — something existentially and radically deeper than a plain desire to change job or take a break from work in the midst of a global pandemic. What it has perhaps demonstrated has been the surfacing of a widespread unconscious desire to abandon the paradigms that govern our neoliberal world. At the most pessimistic of moments, amid global chaos, a flicker of possibility to disentangle oneself from the norms and structures of neoliberal capitalist socio-economic patterns. At the moment when capitalism, for once, seemed vulnerable, as it became existentially threatened by an apocalyptic natural occurrence few could have predicted, the worker felt enabled to react, to retreat, to escape. Other, more naturalistic, survivalist and epicurean impulses took hold, and our ties to the world of work ceased — at least for a moment — to hold as tight a grip as they once did. Ultimately, and regretfully, this did not last. Out of necessity, people returned to work. But for a moment a possibility was discernible. Capitalism's fragility exposed and unleashed an unconscious, mass resignation as people rethought themselves within and outside of the neoliberal capitalist framework, negated the value placed on the labour experience and sought to readdress their own subjectivity, desires and identity as no longer the mere subject of capital. During one of the darkest moments for humanity in living memory, the possibility for an escape emerged in the form of a negation, a subtraction of self from economy. That this has not lasted, nor been fully capitalised on by the Left in any grand or coordinated socio-economic refusal, is not the point. What is important is that, for a moment, something may have been possible. Thoughts of disentanglement and refusal and a pathway toward us unbound from the will and world of work in an exploitative neoliberal capitalist paradigm ruminated.

Disentanglement refers to a reaction against a particular kind of alienation, in the Marxist sense. For Marx, the worker experiences alienation from their humanity as a consequence of their subsumption into the mechanistic workings of capitalism and class society. The working subject under capitalism is no longer considered entirely human, but the sum of the value of their labour. Utopia becomes a world whereby the people are pulled out from the grip of capitalist power, and wherein the workers are reunited with their humanity and agency. I, however, want to speculate that the perpetually suffering human subject (also known as the subject of capitalism) exists now totally alienated from the possibility to escape the codified ontological capitalist system imbued within them. Rather than simply an alienation from their humanity, the subject further suffers from an alienation to their inherent negating capacities, which are synonymous with their potentiality. This disconsolate, pessimistic subject does not want to merely affirm or better the person they are within the context of the world as it exists, they require to escape these parameters and unlock their critical capacities to explore the notion of something else. Disentanglement, then, refers to a desire to unlock a negating dimension through a repudiation or undoing.

To tease out this notion of disentanglement further, we can venture that when a subject cannot change, challenge or attack the external source of their angst and ire, they may instead choose to attack or enact a self-defeating/self-destructive change in themselves in order to alter their position within and against a pervasive, ever fluid and abstract or unattainable target. This attack or denunciation against self is recognisable in three clear directions. The first is the literal, individual-suicidal curtailing of one's own life, an act which has tragically taken the form of an epidemic in recent decades as, for a great number of rational and irrational reasons, people are deciding that finality and closure is preferable to the burden, entropy and suffering brought by continuity. The second is found in the prospect of a world without us: a world without human beings and all of our baggage, where nature can function and thrive in calm seclusion; but also, more cynically, a distinctly human utopian fantasy of our self-removal from the experiential world-as-we-know-it. The third stems from the principle that existence equals suffering and proposes that because suffering is unjustified and to be eradicated, an end to suffering by removing the beings which suffer is desirable. Anti-natalism is not — in theory — a wholly sadistic proposition, but a notionally moral one that questions our propensity to accept suffering when other options are presented. By attributing less pain and suffering to non-existence (as a species), the escape from or negation of existence becomes a justifiable, optimal state — hypothetically at least.[56] Anti-natalism is a thought experiment which mobilises philosophical and existential pessimism against human life as means of reducing the damages which humanity inflicts on both the human the inhuman world(s).

Empirically speaking, the discontinuation of life is warranted as the most pragmatic response to the question of life's burden.

The extinction of the human race, for the anti-natalist, then, is a utopian prospect, culminating in a world without suffering. We cannot, however, overlook the practical and theoretical horrors this would necessitate — namely, a headfirst rush towards fatality. Less nihilistic perhaps, I prefer to consider a further negation in response to the matter and propose that the prospect and capacity to moderate our own exposure to the tangible horrors of the capitalist world emerges through self-destruction and refusal. But first let us circle back to the crux of the problem: existence equals suffering. Reframed in more practicable Marxist terms, and grounded on our present neoliberal constellation, we might instead say, as Berardi has shown, existence equals *work* equals suffering, and attempt to propose a way out of this equation.

It seems, at present, critics and optimists alike are set on a course to find, reveal or propose a utopia that is a world in itself or a world in its own right: something tangible and valued (or more aptly, the product of a series of values). As I teased at the outset: that wonderful, impossible place. After all our pessimistic ruminations and confrontations with the many challenges faced in the even slightly attempted conceptualisation of a utopian endpoint (be that of time or place), it is clear that we need to abandon any optimistic delusion that utopia can be found in our world. Instead, it becomes reasonable to consider utopia as the fundamental negation of this (or any other) world that we can materially be a part of. Further still, rather than as envisioned as a world without us, perhaps it is now even more appropriate to conceive of utopia as the eschatological fantasy of *us without the world*. Utopia, by this arrangement, emerges as the culmination of a self-destructive disentanglement from the material and abstract worlds, which, as Mark Fisher's *Capitalist Realism* (2009) purports, are synonymous with an evolving, impervious and inescapable neoliberal capitalist totality.[57]

As the unwitting subjects and products of a totalising capitalist hegemony, when subjects subsequently challenge themselves, they incidentally rebel against the networks, fluxes and ontological paradigms that codify their understanding and experience of the world. Furthermore, when these same subjects destroy themselves (disentangling themselves from their codified capitalist ties), they bring into question the possibility of enacting a truly radical alternative that otherwise cannot be fully envisaged. Self-destructive activities — and by which I specifically refer to a destruction of a 'self' that is fundamentally tied to capitalist hegemony — negate the affirmationist excessive and productive ideals that are hard-coded within the 'rational' individual, and which serve the material needs of neoliberal capitalism. In this way, self-destruction defies the naturalisation of neoliberal and postmodern values that regulate our behaviours, shape our world and demand our compliance. In so doing, a utopian resonance emerges from this negation, in the removal or escape of the self from world and in the conceptualisation or fantasy of *us* untied from the totalising world as we know it.

CONCLUSION

As Fredric Jameson has described, the postmodern world has brought about a waning of affect that follows the disappearance of the individual subject and the transformation and commodification of human subjects into fragments, embodiments of a virtual deconstruction of the very aesthetic of expression.[58] Postmodern and neoliberal culture in the late twentieth and early twenty-first centuries has vehemently pushed subjects towards alienation, consumption, compulsion and complicity in (or cynical acceptance of) the naturalisation of these negativistic or damaging values. The erasure or dissolution of any meaningful affect or feeling has led to a profound sense of cultural, artistic and political pessimism characterised by detachment. By way of response, the need has emerged for an alternative, a way out: for simply not this. But 'not this' has become fundamentally utopian owing to the complete subsumption of reality into the framework of neoliberal capitalism. The 'will' of the world as the inescapable cause and condition of existential suffering becomes, now, the 'will' of the world of capitalism: Capitalist Realism, Semiocapitalism, No Escape. Utopia becomes the imaginative formulation of ourselves at a remove or subtracted from this world.

Pessimism is borne not entirely of a defeatist concession that all that is and ever will be is lost, but, more accurately, that on our current trajectory, and by virtue of society's sublimation, existence is indeed a very bleak situation. That there exists little hope of change (though hope is not entirely lost) and scant appetite for positivism, reflects the difficulty in imagining, never mind enacting, drastic change in the world. Schopenhauer said that philosophy's purpose is to demonstrate the futility of change in a thoroughly unredeemable world. Marx sought to disprove this, although the ever evolving and totalising capitalist forms of the twentieth and early twenty-first centuries have proven to be stubborn adversaries for Marx's followers. Whilst we may not be able to fully and satisfactorily change the world to our liking, it does not mean that we cannot, at least, speculate and plot a more profound and different approach. From the pessimist's grim vantage point, we are presented with an unflinchingly precise view of the horrors faced in the world. Only from this enlightened position can we (individually and communally) fully expose and confront our world's pernicious cultural and political machinations, and better navigate these treacherous climes. From a pragmatic, pessimistic starting point, the utopian dream becomes the dream of an escape, for one and all, and the fundamental negation of the world.

This is not, however, to idealise the lone agent who, in the dead of night, retreats to their mountaintop chalet, locks the doors and has the temerity to malign others for not having the good sense to get away from it all. Indeed, this kind of privitisation of utopian thought ironically mirrors neoliberalism's focus on the individual as lone agent for change to the detriment of radical, ethical and empathetic collective action, the renunciation of reality and the imagination of the utopian other. To be clear, when discussing utopianism as a fundamental negation of the domain of capitalism, pessimism condemns the appeasement or affirmation of oneself as doing nothing to prevent or change the fundamental, widespread suffering of the present human predicament.

These pages have sought to speculate a pathway from disconsolation towards a utopian *something else* — even if this pathway asserts that we have no choice but to abandon our comforting illusions and leap, headfirst, into a void beyond the secure confines of reason and the world we know. When we do stare into this void, all manner of terror and possibility are conjured as the beckon cry of a great many different utopias all call out from beyond: radicalism and the utopia of our world made better; nihilism and the utopia of a different world; but also, shrouded in melancholy, the chance for estrangement and the disentanglement of the self from the world — the utopia of us without the world.

This utopia is the spectre of an unreachable, intangible eschatological possibility beyond the pale — a haunting, enticing absence that disrupts the somnolence of the familiar world and demarcates the inherent cruelty underpinning its machinations. Utopianism becomes a pessimistic conceit that says 'better' cannot be realised within this ontological plain. Utopianism, then, is a spectral negativism which demands a (hopeful) speculative leap into the void to escape a system whereby any affirmative prospect ('good life' fantasies, reformism or radical invention *within* the world) is a delusion that further embeds and alienates subjects within its confines.

If the only hope for a better or different world, for utopia, is an uncertain passage through negativity, why would we not cling to the established order? Why risk oblivion for the impossible? As the pages of this book have offered, continuity equates to complicity and a self-destructive slow death for all. Although the possibility of escape may be inconceivable, that is because current utopian discourses are infected by a weaponised positivism that maintains the primacy of the very system we seek to overcome. Pessimism does not profess to have the answers, but this does not invalidate its dissident position against the hegemony of capitalist realism. Whilst optimism closes off the possibility for divergence, collective refusal and the embrace of negativity begins the imaginative process of untethering ourselves from and unravelling ontological givens and structural paradigms.

Emmanuel Levinas argued that an 'escape' is manifested as a 'strange disquiet, [that] appears like a condemnation — the most radical one — of the philosophy of ... being'.[59] For Levinas, escape is characterised in a radical disbelief or negation of ontological and tautological givens, it is an escape premised on the confrontation with the horrific 'nausea' of existence and being.[60] Confronted by a similar horror at the abhorrent nature of the world we live in, the disconsolate dreamers seek to escape their collective circumstances through the utopian fantasy. What makes this pessimistic-utopian escapism interesting is that it does not pertain to any sense of optimistic affirmation, release or relief. It is not 'the quest for the marvellous', as Levinas put it, but instead is a distraction that counteracts existential horror with the unbound possibility of uncertainty.[61] For Levinas, 'escape is the need to get out of oneself', to break free of the illusionary stability of self-knowing within this world.[62] Utopia(nism) is the projection of ourselves into negativity, towards a self-destructive/self-abandoning escapist fantasy that breaks the somnolence and suffering of our neoliberal existence. Utopia, then, is the imagined unconceptualisable space beyond absolutes and meaning — it is the actualisation or representation of pure nothing. If that is the case, then where must we go from here — moreover, where can we go — but headfirst into a literal and metaphorical nowhere?

ABOUT THE AUTHOR

Rachid M'Rabty is a writer from the UK. Based in Manchester, Rachid studied English and Contemporary Literatures at Leeds Beckett University before completing his PhD in English at Manchester Metropolitan University. Away from his writing, Rachid works within Higher Education.

Rachid's PhD thesis explored themes of nihilism, self-destruction and transgression as an anti-capitalist fantasy in contemporary British and American fiction.

Rachid is interested in Contemporary Literature and Film, Gothic and Horror Studies, Marxist/Post-Marxist Critical Theory and is currently working on two further projects within these areas.

NOTES/REFERENCES

1 Žižek, S. (2017) *The Courage of Hopelessness*, London, Allen Lane, p. x.
2 Thacker, E. (2012) 'Cosmic Pessimism', *Continent*, 2:2, 66–75, p. 66.
3 Stoneman, E. and Packer, J. (2017) 'No, everything is not all right: Supernatural horror as pessimistic argument', *Horror Studies*, 8:1, pp. 25–43, p. 26.
4 Berlant, L. (2013) *Cruel Optimism*, London, Duke University Press: Žižek, S. (2017) *The Courage of Hopelessness*: Eagleton, T. (2015) *Hope Without Optimism*, London, Yale University Press.
5 Žižek, S. (2017) *The Courage of Hopelessness*, p. xxi.
6 ibid, p. xviii.
7 ibid, p. 290.
8 Berlant, L. (2013) *Cruel Optimism*, p. 1.
9 ibid, p. 3.
10 ibid, p. 3.
11 Eagleton, T. (2015) *Hope Without Optimism*, p. 110.
12 ibid, p. 132.
13 Williams, R. (1989) *The Politics of Modernism*, London, Verso, p. 104.
14 Eagleton, T. (2015) *Hope Without Optimism*, p. 123.
15 ibid, p. 35.
16 Ligotti, T. (2010) *The Conspiracy against the Human Race*, New York, Hippocampus Press.

17 Schopenhauer, A. (1819, 1844) *The World as Will and Representation, vols. 1 & 2*, New York, Dover, 1969.

18 Schopenhauer, A. *The Essential Schopenhauer*, ed. by Wolfgang Schirmacher, New York, Harper Perennial, 2010, p. 1.

19 Critchley, S. (2017) *Notes on Suicide*, London, Fitzcarraldo, p. 72. See also Benatar, D. (2017) *The Human Predicament*, Oxford, Oxford University Press: Cioran, E.M. (1973) *The Trouble with Being Born*, trans. by Richard Howard, London, Penguin, 2020: Thacker, E. (2018) *Infinite Resignation*, London, Repeater.

20 Lukács, G. 'From Goethe and Hegel to Schopenhauer and Nietzsche' (1942), *Marxists.org* [online] <https://www.marxists.org/archive/lukacs/works/1942/goethe-hegel.htm>.

21 Benjamin, W. (1979) 'Surrealism: The Last Snapshot of the European Intelligentsia' in *One-Way Street, and other writings*, London, Verso, 2021, pp. 261–279.

22 Land, N. (1992) *The Thirst for Annihilation: Georges Bataille and Virulent Nihilism*, London, Routledge, p. 9.

23 Wark, M. (2017) 'On Nick Land', *Verso Books*, [online] <https://www.versobooks.com/blogs/3284-on-nick-land>.

24 Brassier, R. (2010) 'Accelerationism', *Moskvax*, [online] <https://moskvax.wordpress.com/2010/09/30/accelerationism-ray-brassier/?fbclid=IwAR1odxHWQd7HHgpbjetDo0jGeYATION9D39jCGbppCxS8x-fJyou239oe_s>.

25 Noys, B. (2012) *The Persistence of the Negative: Critique of Contemporary Continental Theory*, Edinburgh, University of Edinburgh Press, p. 162.

26 ibid, p. 168.

27 van der Lugt, M. (2021) *Dark Matters*, Princeton, NJ, Princeton University Press, p. 409.

28 Dienstag, J. F. (2006) *Pessimism: Philosophy, Ethic, Spirit*, Princeton, Princeton University Press.

29 *Us* (2019) Dir. by Jordan Peele [Film]. Universal Studios.

30 *V for Vendetta* (2005) Dir. by James McTeigue [Film]. Warner Bros. Pictures.

31 Ballard, J.G. (2000) *Super-Cannes*, London, Flamingo

32 Marx, K. (1858) 'Fragment on Machines', in Robin Mackay and Armen Avanessian, eds., *#Accelerate: The Accelerationist Reader*, Falmouth, Urbanomic, 2014, pp. 51–56.

33 Mackay, R. and Avanessian, A. (2014) 'Introduction', in Robin Mackay and Armen Avanessian, eds., *#Accelerate: The Accelerationist Reader*, Falmouth, Urbanomic, 2014, pp. 4–46.

34 Lyotard, J. (1974) *The Libidinal Economy*, trans. By Iain Hamilton Grant, Bloomington, IN, Indiana University Press, 1993, p. 116.

35 Ballard, J.G. (2000) *Super-Cannes*, London, Flamingo, p. 95.

36 Ricoeur, P. (1986) *Lectures on Ideology and Utopia*, ed. G. H. Taylor, New York, Columbia University Press.

37 Žižek, S. (2016) 'The Seeds of Imagination' in Fredric Jameson, *An American Utopia: Dual Power and the Universal Army*, London, Verso, 2016, pp. 267–308.

38 Miéville, C. (2016) 'Limits of Utopia', in Thomas More, *Utopia*, London, Verso, 2016, pp. 11–27.

39 ibid, p. 6.

40 ibid, p. 23.

41 ibid, p. 23.

42 Jameson, F. (2005) *Archaeologies of the Future: The Desire Called Utopia and Other Science Fictions*, London, Verso, p. 217.

43 Miéville, C. (2016) 'Limits of Utopia', pp. 26–7.

44 Noys, B. (2012) *The Persistence of the Negative: Critique of Contemporary Continental Theory*, pp. xi–xii.

45 Ligotti, T. (2003) 'The Town Manager', in *Teatro Grottesco*, London, Virgin Books, 2008, p. 24.

46 ibid, p. 29.

47 ibid, p. 31.

48 ibid, p. 35.

49 Berardi, F. (2009) *The Soul at Work*, Los Angeles, CA, Semiotext(e), pp. 92–3.

50 Fisher, M. (2012) 'Capitalist Realism: Is There Still No Alternative?', *Strike Magazine*, [online] <https://strikemag.org/capitalist-realism-is-there-still-no-alternative>.

51 Fisher, M. (2009) *Capitalist Realism: Is There No Alternative?*, Hants, Zer0 Books.
52 Berardi, F. (2011) *After the Future*, ed. By Gary Genosko and Nicholas Thoburn, Edinburgh, AK Press, p. 58.
53 ibid, pp. 53, 133.
54 Berardi, F. (2019) *Futurability*, London, Verso, p. 71.
55 Berardi, F. (2015) *Heroes*, London, Verso, p. 225.
56 Aldana Reyes, X. and M'Rabty, R. (2019) 'Better not to have been: Thomas Ligotti and the "Suicide" of the Human Race', in *Suicide and the Gothic,* ed. by William Hughes and Andrew Smith, Manchester, Manchester University Press, pp. 124–38.
57 Fisher, M. (2009) *Capitalist Realism: Is There No Alternative?*.
58 Jameson, F. (1991) *Postmodernism: Or, The Cultural Logic of Late Capitalism,* London, Verso, pp. 11, 16.
59 Levinas, E. (1983) *On Escape: De l'évasion,* trans. by Bettina Bergo, Stanford, CA, Stanford University Press, 2003, p. 51.
60 ibid, p. 66.
61 ibid, p. 53.
62 ibid, p. 55.

BIBLIOGRAPHY

Aldana Reyes, Xavier and Rachid M'Rabty (2019) 'Better not to have been: Thomas Ligotti and the "Suicide" of the Human Race', in *Suicide and the Gothic*, ed. by William Hughes and Andrew Smith, Manchester, Manchester University Press, pp. 124–38.

Ballard, J.G. (2000) *Super-Cannes*, London, Flamingo.

Benatar, David (2017) *The Human Predicament*, Oxford, Oxford University Press.

Benjamin, Walter (1979) 'Surrealism: The Last Snapshot of the European Intelligentsia' in *One-Way Street, and other writings*, London, Verso, 2021, pp. 261–279.

Berardi, Franco 'Bifo' (2011) *After the Future*, ed. by Gary Genosko and Nicholas Thoburn, Edinburgh, AK Press.

Berardi, Franco 'Bifo' (2019) *Futurability*, London, Verso.

Berardi, Franco 'Bifo' (2009) *The Soul at Work*, Los Angeles, CA, Semiotext(e).

Berlant, Lauren (2013) *Cruel Optimism*, London, Duke University Press.

Brassier, Ray (2010) 'Accelerationism', *Moskvax* [online] <https://moskvax. wordpress.com/2010/09/30/accelerationism-ray-brassier/?fbclid=Iw AR1odxHWQd7HHgpbjetDo0jGeYATION9D39jCGbppCxS8x-fJyou239oe_s>.

Cioran, E.M. (1973) *The Trouble with Being Born*, trans. by Richard Howard, London, Penguin, 2020.

Critchley, Simon (2017) *Notes on Suicide*, London, Fitzcarraldo.

Dienstag, Joshua Foa (2006) *Pessimism: Philosophy, Ethic, Spirit*, Princeton, Princeton University Press.

Eagleton, Terry (2015) *Hope Without Optimism*, London, Yale University Press.

Fisher, Mark (2012) 'Capitalist Realism: Is There Still No Alternative?', *Strike Magazine*, [online] <https://strikemag.org/capitalist-realism-is-there-still-no-alternative>.

Fisher, Mark (2009) *Capitalist Realism: Is There No Alternative?*, Hants, Zer0 Books.

Jameson, Fredric (2005) *Archaeologies of the Future: The Desire Called Utopia and Other Science Fictions*, London, Verso, 2005.

Jameson, Fredric (1991) *Postmodernism: Or, The Cultural Logic of Late Capitalism*, London, Verso.

Land, Nick (1992) *The Thirst for Annihilation: Georges Bataille and Virulent Nihilism*, London, Routledge.

Levinas, Emmanuel (1983) *On Escape: De l'évasion*, trans. by Bettina Bergo, Stanford, CA, Stanford University Press, 2003

Ligotti, Thomas (2010) *The Conspiracy against the Human Race*, New York, Hippocampus Press.

Lukács, Georg (1942) 'From Goethe and Hegel to Schopenhauer and Nietzsche', *Marxists.org* [online] <https://www.marxists.org/archive/lukacs/works/1942/goethe-hegel.htm>.

Lyotard, Jean-François (1974) *The Libidinal Economy*, trans. By Iain Hamilton Grant, Bloomington, IN, Indiana University Press, 1993.

Mackay, Robin and Armen Avanessian (2014) 'Introduction', in Robin Mackay and Armen Avanessian, eds., *#Accelerate: The Accelerationist Reader*, Falmouth, Urbanomic, 2014, pp. 4–46.

Marx, Karl (1858) 'Fragment on Machines', in Robin Mackay and Armen Avanessian, eds., *#Accelerate: The Accelerationist Reader*, Falmouth, Urbanomic, 2014, pp. 51–66.

Miéville, China (2016) 'Limits of Utopia', in Thomas More, *Utopia*, London, Verso, pp. 11–27.

Noys, Benjamin (2012) *The Persistence of the Negative: Critique of Contemporary Continental Theory*, Edinburgh, University of Edinburgh Press.

Ricoeur, Paul (1986) *Lectures on Ideology and Utopia*, ed. G. H. Taylor, New York, Columbia University Press.

Schopenhauer, Arthur, *The Essential Schopenhauer*, ed. by Wolfgang Schirmacher, New York, Harper Perennial, 2010.

Schopenhauer, Arthur (1819, 1844) *The World as Will and Representation*, vols. 1 & 2, New York, Dover, 1969.

Stoneman, Ethan and Joseph Packer (2017) 'No, everything is not all right: Supernatural horror as pessimistic argument', *Horror Studies*, 8:1, pp. 25–43.

Thacker, Eugene (2012) 'Cosmic Pessimism', *Continent*. 2:2, pp. 66–75.

Thacker, Eugene (2018) *Infinite Resignation*, London, Repeater.

Us (2019) Dir. by Jordan Peele [Film]. Universal Studios.

V for Vendetta (2005) Dir. by James McTeigue [Film]. Warner Bros. Pictures.

van der Lugt, Mara (2021) *Dark Matters*, Princeton, NJ, Princeton University Press.

Wark, McKenzie (2017) 'On Nick Land', *Verso Books* [online] <https://www.versobooks.com/blogs/3284-on-nick-land>.

Williams, Raymond (1989) *The Politics of Modernism*, London, Verso.

Žižek, Slavoj (2016) 'The Seeds of Imagination' in Fredric Jameson, *An American Utopia: Dual Power and the Universal Army*, London, Verso, pp. 267–308.

Žižek, Slavoj (2017) *The Courage of Hopelessness*, London, Allen Lane.

CULTURE, SOCIETY & POLITICS

Contemporary culture has eliminated the concept and public figure of the intellectual. A cretinous anti-intellectualism presides, cheer-led by hacks in the pay of multinational corporations who reassure their bored readers that there is no need to rouse themselves from their stupor. Zer0 Books knows that another kind of discourse — intellectual without being academic, popular without being populist — is not only possible but already flourishing. Zer0 is convinced that in the unthinking, blandly consensual culture in which we live, critical and engaged theoretical reflection is more important than ever before.

If you have enjoyed this book, why not tell other readers by posting a review on your preferred book site.

You may also wish to subscribe to our Zer0 Books YouTube Channel.

Bestsellers from Zer0 Books include:

Poor but Sexy
Culture Clashes in Europe East and West
Agata Pyzik
How the East stayed East and the West stayed West.
Paperback:978-1-78099-394-2 ebook: 978-1-78099-395-9

An Anthropology of Nothing in Particular
Martin Demant Frederiksen
A journey into the social lives of meaninglessness.
Paperback: 978-1-78535-699-5 ebook: 978-1-78535-700-8

In the Dust of This Planet
Horror of Philosophy vol. 1
Eugene Thacker
In the first of a series of three books on the Horror of Philosophy,
In the Dust of This Planet offers the genre of horror as a way of
thinking about the unthinkable.
Paperback: 978-1-84694-676-9 ebook: 978-1-78099-010-1

The End of Oulipo?
An Attempt to Exhaust a Movement
Lauren Elkin, Veronica Esposito
Paperback: 978-1-78099-655-4 ebook: 978-1-78099-656-1

Capitalist Realism
Is There No Alternative?
Mark Fisher
An analysis of the ways in which capitalism has presented itself
as the only realistic political-economic system.
Paperback: 978-1-84694-317-1 ebook: 978-1-78099-734-6

Rebel Rebel
Chris O'Leary
David Bowie: every single song. Everything you want to know,
everything you didn't know.
Paperback: 978-1-78099-244-0 ebook: 978-1-78099-713-1

Cartographies of the Absolute
Alberto Toscano, Jeff Kinkle
An aesthetics of the economy for the twenty-fi rst century.
Paperback: 978-1-78099-275-4 ebook: 978-1-78279-973-3

Malign Velocities
Accelerationism and Capitalism
Benjamin Noys
Long listed for the Bread and Roses Prize 2015, *Malign Velocities*
argues against the need for speed, tracking acceleration
as the symptom of the ongoing crises of capitalism.
Paperback: 978-1-78279-300-7 ebook: 978-1-78279-299-4

Babbling Corpse
Vaporwave and the Commodifi cation of Ghosts
Grafton Tanner
Paperback: 978-1-78279-759-3 ebook: 978-1-78279-760-9

New Work New Culture
Work we want and a culture that strengthens us
Frithjof Bergmann
A serious alternative for humankind and the planet.
Paperback: 978-1-78904-064-7 ebook: 978-1-78904-065-4

Romeo and Juliet in Palestine
Teaching Under Occupation
Tom Sperlinger
Life in the West Bank, the nature of pedagogy and the role of a
university under occupation.
Paperback: 978-1-78279-637-4 ebook: 978-1-78279-636-7

Color, Facture, Art and Design
Iona Singh
This materialist definition of fine art develops guidelines for
architecture, design, cultural studies, and ultimately, social
change.
Paperback: 978-1-78099-629-5 ebook: 978-1-78099-630-1

Sweetening the Pill
or How We Got Hooked on Hormonal Birth Control
Holly Grigg-Spall
Has contraception liberated or oppressed women?
Sweetening the Pill breaks the silence on the dark side of hormonal contraception.
Paperback: 978-1-78099-607-3 ebook: 978-1-78099-608-0

Why Are We the Good Guys?
Reclaiming Your Mind from the Delusions of Propaganda
David Cromwell
A provocative challenge to the standard ideology that Western power is a benevolent force in the world.
Paperback: 978-1-78099-365-2 ebook: 978-1-78099-366-9

The Writing on the Wall
On the Decomposition of Capitalism and its Critics
Anselm Jappe, Alastair Hemmens
A new approach to the meaning of social emancipation.
Paperback: 978-1-78535-581-3 ebook: 978-1-78535-582-0

Neglected or Misunderstood
The Radical Feminism of Shulamith Firestone
Victoria Margree
An interrogation of issues surrounding gender, biology, sexuality, work and technology, and the ways in which our imaginations continue to be in thrall to ideologies of maternity and the nuclear family.
Paperback: 978-1-78535-539-4 ebook: 978-1-78535-540-0

For video content, author interviews and more, please subscribe to our YouTube channel:

zer0repeater

Follow us on social media for book news, promotions and more:

Facebook: ZeroBooks

Instagram: @zero.books

Twitter: @Zer0Books

Tik Tok: @zer0repeater